Beautifully Bruised

The pain behind the smile

Latreka Jones

Beautifully Bruised

Copyright © 2019 by Latreka Jones.

All rights reserved. Printed in the United States of America. No part of this book may be used or reproduced in any manner whatsoever without written permission except in the case of brief quotations embodied in critical articles or reviews.

This book is based on a true-life story. Names, characters, businesses, organizations, places, events and incidents either are the product of the author's imagination or are used fictitiously. Any resemblance to actual persons, living or dead, events, or locales is entirely coincidental.

For information contact:
beautifullybruisedlj@gmail.com

Book and Cover design by La Treka Jones

ISBN: 9781096597179

First Edition: May 2019

Dedication

Dedicated to the ones who have impacted my life by their presence throughout the years of my life. In which includes my sons Courtlend Anderson and Journey Williams. Mama loves you and forever will. Rosie Lee Jones and Sylvia Lee Jones your genuine true love remains remarkable. Thank you for setting a fine example for me to follow. You allowed me to explore and be creative while becoming the woman who God has called me to be. My prayer is for my life to have the same fulfilled mission on those who seek to follow my spiritual path.

CONTENTS

Beautifully Bruised	1
Introduction	5
The Start of Forever	12
A Mother's Touch	23
The Journey Back Home	35
A New Start	41
Finding Myself	52
The Loan	62
The Knockout	67
Final Words	72
About Author	77
More about the Author	78
Motivational Coach	79
Special Moments Pictures	80 - 83
Divine Strategies from God	84
Special Recognition	85
Inspirational Scriptures / Don't Quit Poem	92 - 94
References - Acknowledgements	95 - 96
Note Page	98 -101

Introduction

The Understanding

SINCE I've put God first in my life, I'm very thankful he never gave up on me. All the times the devil tried to bring me evil, God always turned it around for my good. God is so consistent and patient, that sometimes I'm speechless how he loves me like he does. This endless love continues to fascinate and encourages me to seek after him even more. This is why I look forward to worship and going to church to learn as much as I can about him. Over fifteen years ago, I joined the Potter's House Church of Dallas.

The incomparable and undeniable Bishop TD Jake's, for the first time preached to my drowning soul. During this season in my life, I was engulfed in an abusive toxic relationship that turned into depression and isolation. I've never seen or heard anyone articulate the bible in the way Bishop TD Jake's is anointed to do. I recall listening to his sermons on television and tears begin to rapidly fall on the sides of my face, all while dealing with the low valleys of life.

I will never forget, the sermon "Woman Thou Art Loosed" I heard that day. It literally changed my perception and direction for the rest of my life, I once depended on and glorified worldly things. Thankfully my taste changed to quenching my new found thirst for Godly things.

This encounter allowed me to step out of darkness and peek behind the curtains, for the first time to take a deeper glimpse towards the light of God. I wanted to remain depressed by having to deal with so much adversity. Even with the bad decisions I decided to make on my own. But my inner spirit from within would not allow me to remain consumed. It's really a personal choice in how you tend to perceive opposition.

You can either use it as a deterrent to make you feel defeated or as motivation to continue to keep fighting for your breakthrough even more. I would like to personally encourage you to keep moving closer towards your mark! Even with the setbacks and challenges you are dealing with. Life can keep you in constant limbo with vast feelings and mishaps. The good news is that you are not alone. God knows and cares about what you are going through. He will never leave your side. Even when it doesn't seem like he is with you. Just remember to continue to trust in him and keep the faith. It's interesting how our psychological minds can be mentally loud at times with so many distractions. I've learned how to calm my loud thoughts even in chaotic situations.

After studying psychology, for over five years, research has proven positive dialogue can enhance your brain. By using these practical solutions I've been free from my mental anguish which started when I consistently released the negative thoughts I perceived in my mind.

Due to refocusing my thoughts, and actions it helped me to eventually defeat life oppositions, while escaping and surviving my toxic ten-year domestic relationship. I remember saying, God, why did you allow me to survive all the drama and trauma I endured.

However, little did I know, all that I had survived wasn't really about me. After going through a divorce, losing my home, money, assets and dealing with child molestation. Nearly everything I held on to with a high regard, God allowed it all to be taken away. Even while I was suffering with what was happening to me emotionally, physically and financially. God was crushing me spiritually on the inside for what was to come. It continued until I let go of the plans I had for my life, and fully begin to trust the greater plans he had for me. Although I couldn't see this at the time, or even understood and grasp the concept of it all. It was such a humbling experience that I will never forget.

Recently I've been thinking about my last aggressive knockout and how it felt when the world tried to take away and categorize my life was simply heartbreaking. But God knows how and when to step right in for his children. Clearly in an instant moment of time he turned back the hands of darkness that had entered in to destroy my life.

In my forty-three years of living, I've never seen the righteous forsaken. My One hundred- and one-years old grandmother always reminds me, God may not come when you want him, but he is still always right on time. I couldn't do anything but agree with the truth that she shared with me. God is truly faithful, even when we may not be deserving.

While visiting my grandmother on a regular basis, I enjoy spending quality time with her. Listening to centuries worth of wisdom always leaves me intrigued to know more, especially since I lost my mother a few years ago. My life has never been the same since her soul departed from this earth and it's of my deepest pains. During this time, I constantly reminded myself, she may be absent in the body but present with the Lord.

It's not hardly a day that doesn't pass, I don't think about her. As I'm sharing my heart about her, I can't stop my tears from building up because it's a pain that's difficult to explain, unless you have personally witnessed it for yourself.

My grandmother tells me death is something you can never become acquainted with. Living to be her age, she has buried three out of four children. So therefore, I strongly cherish the times we share. She makes me feel like I'm hanging out with a close girlfriend from high school.

It seems we both enjoy hanging out with each other. Sometimes she tells me, to come pick her up so we can go somewhere. Our main locations here in Texas are thrifty store shopping and she loves going out to eat at buffet places.

My grandmother and I love talking over a nice cup of freshly brewed hot coffee and lunch. She starts most of her conversations with random things that cross her mind. Then before you know it, she says something funny, that I can't resist to suddenly laugh at. She has a special sense of humor that helps to ease your day. She lives by saying, you can't allow anything to worry you. Therefore, since she has lived biblical years of age, it would be wise for me to follow her advice.

Being a single mother of two sons with a vast age differences and experiences, my oldest is twenty-three years old and the youngest is six years old. At times, I'm living in two different worlds. But God gives me the strength to get through it. My youngest son Journey is considered a special needs child that requires a tremendous amount of responsibilities.

He once suffered seizures and couldn't walk and still to this day the doctors can't explain why. Journey likes to scream and make random loud noises at times and in spite of these conditions, it has taught me how to create balance while having to constantly multi-task. Even while constant noise may be all around you, that doesn't have to define or justify your inner mental volume inside of you.

You can control it and not having it to control you. It helps to keep some type of positive reinforcement of energy flowing. You can create this atmosphere by using positive music and preparing personal memory notes for yourself.

But I'm very thankful, I didn't faint and held on for dear life to see what his creative strategic unique personal masterpiece would be for my life. It was only by his saving grace and mercy that I survived all of life's vicious traps.

That involved false accusations, persecution, abusive relationships, depression, isolation and grief. My life could have easily been another statistical tragedy story. While many others sadly are. But God gave me a purpose he trusted me to fulfill. In which required me to survive to be able to share my story, in hopes of helping others to heal for his glory!

CHAPTER 1

The Start of Forever

My life first changed in high school; I became involved with a very abusive man. When you're young and still learning the ins and outs of life, you never know what signs to look for in a relationship. I never had a father figure growing up. I found it strange that this man was so interested in me. I was this young teenager that was very plain, in fact I occasionally played with dolls. While he was very flamboyant and seem to love living the fast life. Since he showed great interest in me, I started to date him not knowing this will soon become a very abusive controlling relationship, with my high school sweetheart that would last nearly 10 years. He would give me black eyes, dragged me on the ground in front of his friends and even rip my clothes off. He was a very angry guy who manipulated woman. His previous girlfriend busted my windows out, and he would sometimes leave me on the highway in other towns, if we were out and he thought other men were flirting with me. He was so controlling that I couldn't come outside if his friends came over to visit him. It was a time I thought I couldn't get out of this relationship and he would eventually kill me after he pulled a gun on me.

My closest friend at the time stop being my friend because of his actions. She feared he was going to kill me, but I stayed with him anyway. I ended up becoming pregnant with our first child. He even attacked me and threatened me while pregnant and immediately after birth. I can remember like it was yesterday, the times I use to state to him that I was hungry, he would hit me in my stomach.

Even the times I would try to call it quits with him. He would tell me that doesn't mean I'm calling it quits with you. From public fights to kicking in my front door because he found out I was on a date, with someone else during our time apart. I still feared for my life. I remember even jumping off my upstairs balcony in fear to save my life and to get away from this toxic relationship.

For this to be my first relationship it was extremely unhealthy. Needlessly to say, I got caught up in the scheme of things, and I allowed what should have been only a temporary situation, turn into a long-term misery of episodes that grew into a heaviness of bondage of situations. Here I go again, walking into another trap of misery.

I just remember visiting my therapist and having her tell me, I've never seen a man constantly pick you up to only bring you back down. This was her statement after I shared full details with her of what my husband at the time was doing to me. She was right, he was doing that exact thing to me. This man who swept me off my feet, with all the charm you could ask for, expensive gifts, a car, and didn't want me to work, was just another form of control. As if my heart & soul needed anymore ICU types of emotional and trauma episodes.

Over time I felt like I was slipping away emotionally and mentally. I was losing the desire to move forward. I felt so emotionally drained. It wasn't until I started visiting a church called the Potter's House in Dallas. I started to feel engaged in life again. A pastor by the name of TD Jake's preached on a message called "Woman Thou Art Loose". From this day forward, I started visiting this church and listening more to this type of messages and my life was never the same. I found a new love for Jesus through this ministry. I've always had a special love for Jesus, even since I was a young little girl. My brother asked me one day, who you want to be when you grow up. I said Jesus!

I have always been amazed by his fascinating power; I simply just loved him, without no one teaching me about him. I could even see special images of Jesus that I couldn't explain. Bishop Jake's allowed me to tap back in to my fascination of Jesus, with his ministry. He explained the bible so well, even a little child could understand. I had never experienced this type of revelation before. It provided a foundation that kept my mind balanced through the many pitfalls. That I was facing with my perspective & outlook on life. Although I became renewed through the process of it all.

After this long abusive heartbreaking relationship, I suffered great pain with our only son. While realizing the man I been dating had impregnated his neighbor, coworker and even another individual. Not in that order, but in these categories. I begin to take another deep soul search of who I had become. Our only son started acting out more severely. He numerously ran away from home. He then started getting in trouble in school and getting expelled in elementary school. Even having to go to turning point alternative school. For knowing how to operate through filter systems and having unappropriated behavior and even getting stabbed and needing stitches. Since he was a very smart kid in honors, his teachers tried to work with him as much as possible. Eventually his father turned him against me, while my mother at the time was very sick. I was faced with ongoing accusations and needed to hire an attorney to represent me for family court.

Since his father at the time wasn't really there for him, I knew he was plotting something against me. I had people who witnessed his manipulation tactics and how he managed to get the things he wanted. My son would come home and say mom don't worry about him. He didn't at the time like how his father was talking about me. He even made a broken promise to buy our son a car, if he moved in with him.

I knew his father intentions wasn't good, (he was only trying to be remove from the $10,000 in back child support). Soon after court proceeding started, after so much tearing down in court, and he turned my son against me, emotional wise, I dropped the previous balance he owed me and didn't pursue any more for my sanity remaining. I was so emotionally drained and exhausted.

Afterwards my son became estranged towards me. He almost seems like he was brainwashed as if something had taken over his mind. My mother when she was living always told me, she knew something but she was scared to tell me. Unfortunate, after I always asked her, she never did tell me before she passed.

Later on my son with this new identity of he's betrayed and tried to curse me. I then knew this child had been brainwashed and severely changed. It was no longer wise to pursue and fight for him, as I was desperately trying to do. The words shared broke my will and my spirit. Even counsel advised me not to pursue him until he came to me himself. Especially while I was grieving the death of my mother.

In regards to my oldest son and whom he was surrounded by at a very impressionable time of his life. In which where he was supposed to be staying with his father at the time. That could have easily affected his current life and early to late teenage years of high school. I later found out it was a twist to the story and who was also secretly influencing his actions. I was told and received evidence that my estranged sibling made false reports to CPS pertaining to me.

These lies included secretly enrolling my son into college without my permission. After my oldest son high school graduation. This should have been a special moment to share with him embarking into a new milestone for college. Especially by giving birth to him and raising him the majority of his life. No one in their correct mind frame, should try to take over and take these special bonding moments away from any parent.

I shortly found out after visiting my son and helping to prepare him for school, his financial paperwork records showed he was listed as an orphan for college. I was shocked to read this since it wasn't true. I was surprised that someone would stoop so low and take these types of actions. This is why I have to put my trust in the Lord, and not my own understanding on others true motives.

In the past I had to speak with her to confront her on her out of boundaries conduct, she was utilizing towards our relationship. At that time, I previously had to tell her not to take my son to an out of state trip to California with her colleagues. While later on, I found out she took him to California in spite of me telling her not to. My son later on dropped out of college and moved to California pursuing his music rap dream. Eventually he got involved with some trouble on different occasions, which lead him going to the hospital. I believe granting him access and exposure to these types of freedom lifestyles, contributed to what he experienced.

This should have never occurred if my wishes as his mother would have been respected and adhered to. At this point and time, I felt I had to take some form of action, against what was trying to destroy our relationship.

I had begun to talk to God more about how and what to do. I believe God told me to step back and continue to focus on his will, and he would fight my battles. The continuation of this type of hurt was really unbelievable, especially pertaining to a sibling.

She wasn't aware my son nearly acted out and sometimes ran away when he had emotional triggers. Mostly my mother and I knew this, since we were the ones that mostly raised him. It would have been nice if she would have asked before making drastic decisions regarding my teenage son at the time.

That's why we should truly just let go, and let God! Even when he ran away from home again, during his teenage years, which was a police hunt looking for him. My sister never answered the phone when I tried to call her. At the time I was just trying to call everyone I could to help look for him.

But when the police called his father whom he was supposed to be staying with, his father shared, his mother had picked him up from a gas station and he was taken to my sibling house. I begin to think back.

When I had to calm down my mother, while she was upset about her health situation. My mom was ill at the time and all I wanted to do was help her calm her spirit. Since after all, she was my mother and was there for me when she could be. I didn't want any more negativity energy to disturb her mind, while she was going through having to deal with her sickness and being hospitalized. This is the calmness I needed.

After this time, I found my sister connection with my son to be completely out of her boundaries and control. It seems she was trying to take own my identity as his mother. Since she never been married or had kids of her own. Maybe she was trying to fill something that was missing in her life. I remember her purchasing expensive gifts and my son receiving ear piercing and tattoos, while he was supposed to been in his father care. As if she was trying to buy his love and affection in a distorted type of way.

I had my son in honors courses throughout junior high, since he is a very intelligent kid. I find it interesting someone would be content with this type of character or division created with his parents.

This is why it's important to know the fruit of a person's spirit. It will help you to determine who a person really is and what spiritually they may be connected to.

After the emotional damage was done to my family, I never received any type of remorse or apologetic actions from her, even his father eventually apologized for what happened.

By the grace of God, I did accept his apology, and we have tried to be sensible towards each other and move forward with our separate lives.

I still had to tell her to stop enabling my son, who is now grown and was living in her place. I don't understand how someone not be able to understand, if you are not helping him maybe you are the enabler. This is why it is important to do what God has given you to do. If you were not called or properly assigned to do something, then you simply may be disregarding and operating out of order, and causing more harm than good. Sometimes we can get in our own way, when we should be allowing God to be God. After all, he created all of us, and knows what's best for us all.

Emotionally it all became too much to deal with and I know this heartbreak and devastation of my child lead to my next bad choice. I was left so broken with my reality.

I had become vulnerable in some ways. Trying to fix & repair my broken heart with any tool, I could find in the toolbox. This led me to quickly meeting my ex-husband, who enticed me with his words, and bought me nearly anything I asked for.

I remember him giving me his debit card and telling me to go shopping for a handbag I wanted. I thought I was dreaming, due to all the other hell I was dealing with my custody battles and false accusations claims. I just remember we would talk all hours of the day and night. I thought it was the validation that the little girl inside of me was looking for.

CHAPTER 2

A Mother's Touch

My mother was a very strong insightful woman. Until she became stricken with sickness. She battled with cancer 3 different times, and it hurt me to watch her endure so much pain. But her final words to me, one night late in her hospital room. I asked her how was she was feeling. She mentioned on a 10 scale, as if she was going up on an elevator, and labeled it as a scale of 7 or 8. I could tell her medicine was kicking in, and as I was getting ready to leave.

I just remember her saying, I love you. I replied to her back, I love you too. Not knowing these words would be our final words here in this earthly dwelling. I've learned and continue to learn so much from her touch in my life. Its things I will remember for a lifetime and never forget. Precious fun memories we shared. I remember many days I would call her on my auditions, and she never hesitated to encourage me and become my cheerleader. While waiting to see if I landed the role. I will never forget; I had an audition for a commercial in Dallas Texas.

After narrowing down the full room to only one component. A beautiful blue-eyed Dallas Cowboy Cheerleader and I remained in a quiet room. I just waited on the results that were chosen for the-commercial. I made a quick call to my mother, who we called "Sivie". She immediately answered the phone, and asked how did it go? I told her; I was going against a Dallas Cowboy Cheerleader.

She responded with, give it all you got, and realize you came along way for this kind of opportunity. I realized she was absolutely right. I thought about my mother and me going to Walmart, to pick out my workout outfit I was auditioning in. Including the time and investment I put in my career, to have these types of opportunities. So the casting director called us out to audition for one more final time. In order to choose whom they will finally select for the only role.

I remembered him whispering to me while I was walking back in the auditioning room. They do like you, but you need to show more excitement. I instantly reverted back to what my mother told me, and I told him, you got it!

Waiting 10 minutes or so that seemed like a lifetime at the time. The Dallas Cowboy Cheerleader and I were the only ones again, in a back room for their final selection. I didn't know what to expect, I just knew I gave it my all. It's amazing during these times how fear and anxiety loves to creep up on you. If you are not careful, you would allow fear and anxiety get the best of you. I think it's normal and healthy to be a little apprehensive.

As long as you don't allow it to consume you. When you know you have done the best you can do, you should be able to rest on that alone. If you have talked to God about it with prayer and supplication, he is not the kind of father that focuses on keeping good things away from his children. He said he will give the heart of our desires, if it's in his will. I've grown to learn even if things don't come my way as expected, his rejection is simply just protection.

Jesus will not keep a good thing from happening. This is where we have to strengthen our faith and just trust him while going through the process. This is definitely a learning process. I notice with my walk with the Lord,

I learned more and more as I grow older with maturity of time. Learning to trust the process verses the progress isn't always easy, but it does make sense. Needless to say, after trying to keep calm sitting in the back room. I begin to hear my heartbeat through my clothes. I glanced over across from me, the Dallas Cowboy Cheerleader, was smiling in her uniform.

I begin to smile and look away. While encouraging myself, to keep the faith. I believed I also have what it takes. So no matter what, I was going to wait and see what the end result would be. I was just honored to be in the room, making historic connections with a Dallas Cowboy Cheerleader.

So as we both were quietly awaiting, the door abruptly swung open. It seems like the room got quiet, if that was even possible. It was the same guy that gave me more advice when he entered the room previously. We both looked up towards his direction. It seemed like that was the longest walk in history, with him heading towards our direction. I just remember him stopping by to speak with her first.

I'm thinking to myself I'm about to find out the final truth, what we both been waiting for. I heard him tell her, thank you for coming out! I just remember grabbing my heart in shock, with the news I just heard! I think I was moving in slow motion clearly about to burst in tears. He shortly walked over to me, and said congratulations you have been chosen! He grabbed my hand with a firm handshake, and asked me to follow him to the back. My soul was literally leaping for joy! I couldn't stop smiling.

I believe I even had a tear in the corner of my eye, while meeting many major executives and shaking their hands. They shared with me I did well. I literally could have fainted on the floor.
I tried my best to keep my composure at such an exciting time in my life.

Afterwards I remember leaving their office heading to my car overwhelmed with joy and enormous amount of gratification. For not giving up, and believing in myself. Even with all costs, no matter what my challenges and obstacles were. So I proceeded to call my mother on my cell phone. She answered, and I said I got it! She immediately started screaming! She would always tell me; God will make a way somehow. She would also say; God is an instant God.

I didn't grow up with much. But I love my grandmother and mother because they did the best with what they had. I have always felt loved. I never knew what it was like to not be wanted. I think this is why I struggled with my young child being abandoned. It felt like being in a foreign country and trying to learn and adapt to a new culture. I'm so glad my son normally has a positive spirit. In some kind of way in his young mind, he was eventually able to accept that loss and move on with a smile.

He even told me, mama, daddy may not love me, but I still love him. This was a real tear jerker for me. It was difficult for me to keep it together. That a child at such a tender age has to rationalize this type of feeling. I'm actually inspired by him. If he can still love through the spirit of abandonment, than so can I.

I will take a piece out of his life and use it for my own personal story. In life you will have setbacks and detours. I actually have experienced so many; I find myself at times feeling ok with it. Then at other times I feel as if I just want to disappear. I have witnessed the more you pursue living for Jesus, the more the enemy will try to attack you. That's because I will always continue to keep my heart for loving Jesus.

As I am growing more into my forties, I am realizing that at this age it's an interesting blend of milestones. You realize what you want and what you don't. The confidence level at this age becomes spectacular. It's easier to say no, and knowing you don't have to feel guilty about it. I am willing to accept who I am, while evolving to become the woman I'm destined to be. I enjoy reflecting in my quiet moments in life. I have made my mistakes, but I have always applied myself. I try to do the best I can.

I can see my life is shifting. Once I would always like to be on the move. I still do at times, however not like in my thirties and twenties. I believe I have become more in tune with my physical and spiritual body. Where the pace has taken a different rhythm.

I don't worry about what I can't change but only work towards what I can. One can capture and learn honestly what the serenity prayer truly means. Life is to short and precious to worry about past mistakes. The only thing you can try to do is move on from them. Hopefully learn from them and not repeat them. Life can be an exciting adventure, with God first and being yourself while he leads you.

Although I have always thought it's a great mystery at the same time. I hear certain stories of tragedies that simply breaks my heart and become quiet of why this happen. I certainly see why God says to lean not to your own understanding. Due to it's just some things that probably will never make any kind of sense. I think this is why the serenity prayer has so much merit and substance in its wording.

Everything we need in life is inside the Holy bible. It reveals all that we need to know as believers about this world. Its some stories that moves me to tears, at times laughing, while others have me sitting still. It is the anchor for human souls to hold onto for all points of reference.

My 101-year-old grandmother, would use the words, God has been good to you. I have enough common sense for a blessed lady of longevity, to adhere to what she says. God has not left her this long on this earth for nothing. She has wisdom that I have never ever seen before. I have learned so much from her throughout the years of my life.

She has majority raised me. Since I never knew my father, my mother would leave me with my grandmother often. To this day, I admire her strength, wisdom, style and grace. She still has poise and definition that's unchangeable. I study her and pay close attention to her details and conversations. She normally has a joke, fact or simply a unique nugget she drops in my life that I can carry and study from. I love the balance in how she carries her perspective in life.

She would always tell me, Treka don't let things worry you. I use to be the type, I would easily allow things to bother me. I must admit, as my seasons change, as I get older, I've learned to lay things down more. Especially if it's nothing extreme and dangerous to my personal life. Once I see something and or someone is not healthy for me, I learn to move from it.

She tells me to this day, you might give out, but don't never give up! This is so true. It may be times you just have to stop what you are doing and reevaluate yourself and your situation. Even sometimes you may have to even cry. I've Studied Psychology for nearly five years.

It is healthy to release yourself from situations that you know without thinking about it, can be harmful to your future. Close any open door that can trigger you into depression, anxiety, or any type of unhealthy disorder. Take a time out break and do what you need to release those negative thoughts from your mind.

Since I have been in abusive relationships, it took me a while to learn how to just leave. I use to have a problem with saying no. Therefore I would take on more obligations than I should. I must admit slightly in some ways I still do the same thing.

But only for people and things that are important to me. You just can't waste your time and energy on everything. Balance is the key. Many may not understand your vision and plans that God has for you. Sometimes you may have to discover this alone.

It seems when God calls you into your true element and position in life, you have to be in a special place spiritually, where you can hear clearly from him. A place of spiritual freedom, where you are not connected to any outside distractions are people that can hinder you.

Block the pop ups and keep going! In order to walk with God, you really have to have your mind made up. Your decisions and thoughts have to be solid and pure with his. If not the pressures and pain of attacks in life can easily knock you from your promise.

My pastor would always say, in order to get what God has for you, it's definitely going to cost you something. Much is given where much is required. This can appear easily said than done. Especially when you are going through the fire and trials of life.

To this day, I can say my mother was very inspiring and encouraging to me towards my acting career. She was really a laid-back type of mother. She allowed me to have free will on my thought process. She really didn't intervene too much.

Maybe because she knew God would work it all out for his glory. And she was right. I really think my mother had a prophet calling on her life. It's like she could see things before they happened. I never will forget, once we visited a church event.

She sat out in the car, while she waited for me to go inside. Once I came back out, she asked me a few questions. Then she told me she never wanted to return back there again. I didn't understand why she would make that comment. Not until shortly later, that same church was on the news.

The reporting found the pastor guilty of raping teenager girls. From that very moment it confirmed the difference of insight that my mother had. I noticed she had a great connection with people. She loved giving her close friends fun nicknames. She had a great sense of humor and loved to laugh. But she also wasn't anyone you wanted to take her kindness for weakness.

Even while going out with her to garage sales that we both loved to do often. She would ask me to pray for people. I didn't understand why, but now I do. I believe this was a calling on my life that she could see back then.

She would also tell me, Treka, just because you understand things, doesn't mean common sense is so common. She also gave me advice, to not put majority of my time in my kids, and none in myself. And she was right again.

As life begins to unveil more, I can understand why she gave me this wise advice. It helped to clarify what I witnessed later in life. I couldn't picture myself trying to take over someone else impactful position as a mother. So my mother wisdom helped me to process the outcome.

CHAPTER 3

The Journey Back Home

Going back to my grandmother and our numerous conversations. I always recalled saying "Life is not Easy". In this journey nothing worth having comes easy. This morning I was praying and talking to God. I shared with him; I have a made-up mind to live for God. No matter who come or go. It is always going to be something we will have to deal with in this world.

Life at times can be a fight on every hand. You have to fight sometimes just to rise above and not fall to the many downfalls. I have learned you really can't be consumed by the naysayers and people that think they know you, but really don't. If you listen to them, you will be disappointed every time. I truly know the reason why we must keep our trust in God. It helps to keep your mind clear and not easily moved or concerned with what people do or say. I have always found God to be an anchor like no other. He has a way of keeping you, even when you don't want to be kept.

With all the major distractions in this world, I'm so glad he thought enough of his servants to give us a place of rescue. God has already overcome the world. So he knows all the troubles we would endure. Especially trying to live right for me. The trials and tribulation are real, and no one is exempt from it. God is a God of second chances.

He is so forgiving and loving. He is the true definition of a redeemer. For example, I have seen so many times in my personal life where he has made a way for me. I've seen times where I didn't have enough funding resources to fulfill a need. Even though I have faced these challenges, uncertain what will occur. Thankfully it worked out! This is what helped me cross many barriers in my life.

 As I can recall I lived in Atlanta Georgia, at the time of possible career opportunities as an aspiring actress. I was over 800 miles away from my family. I was the only one living there without any family near. I knew it was imperative to make wise choices and stay focused for why I was there. I joined a church called New Birth with senior late pastor Bishop Eddie Long. I remember when I needed some financial help to travel back home to Texas. My oldest son and I were at church on a weekend playing sports with other church members. I mentioned to Bishop Eddie Long, that we were trying to get back home. He only asked one question, "Were we driving or flying back." Afterwards while enjoying playing basketball, Bishop Eddie Long said he would be over shortly to speak with me.

Bishop shortly came over in his basketball gear, to confirm all the information was correct about us trying to return back to our home town. He asked me to go meet his assistant in the church foyer office in 20 minutes or so. He proceeded with a hug and went back to the basketball court to continue his game.

I just remember being in shock how helpful he was towards us. He was a very generous helpful man and I will never forget how he helped us to arrive back to Texas safely. He provided more than what I expected. Therefore that brought me even more peace of mind, while driving back to Texas by myself.

I found being separated from everything I knew of, allowed me to enhance my walk with the Lord. I was able to tap into his goodness without any distractions. I also realized when you are that many miles away, you really have to lean on him and trust him. It was the best experience I've ever had. I landed a few auditions. I received a 2nd call back for a Salt & Pepa along with Kid & Play production, but do to funding it was postponed. That can sometime happens, in the entertainment business. I received a chance to really meet some outstanding people while developing and enriching spiritual walk with my father Jesus. I lived in Atlanta nearly a year or so. I was very thankful for my uncle Joe who came down to help me with my young son at the time. I didn't feel comfortable leaving him in a new state with a new babysitter.

So my uncle assistance brought great support to us. Joe even landed an awesome job while being in Atlanta. Although I received several chances to audition for people such as 112, Jagged Edge, Salt & Pepa and Kid & Play. I overall enjoyed the sweet spirit of Douglasville Georgia that I would never forget. In my personal opinion it was a great city to live in, where people didn't mine helping each other.

Due to many industry people that reside there, it also provides endless career opportunities as well. However, when my lease was up, I decided to relocate back to Texas. It was a bittersweet decision.

It was difficult for me to leave a city that I grew to love. Later on, I realized it was a good, I decided to move back to my hometown Texas. Since I found out my mother was becoming ill. In life we are going to experience outcomes. Some may be happy and others may be disappointing. One thing I have noticed is that life is something that never remains fully the same. It is always a constant change happening. In some type of form or fashion. The only thing I realized that's steady and never changing is God.

He is the only consistent thing that forever lasts throughout eternity. I use to not understand why people have to age, die and change. I also wondered why nearly every element in life do the same thing. But the reality is that's just life. Maybe this is why people be trying to keep things the way they formally were.

Women and men that begin to age find themselves trying to add features to themselves to age backwards. For example, this can be from facelifts and hair implants including enhancing their physical appearances. I think its beauty in aging gracefully.

I know certain situations may need additional assistance, however if not, I believe in trying to take care of yourself and being content with how God has made you to be. The beauty in acceptance of who you really are speaks confidence. This is something a person can carry when they enter into a room and while opening their mouth when they speak. Learning to love yourself and accepting who you are is what makes life interesting and meaningful.

 For example, when my mother began to age and started feeling ill at times, she would make the comment when she looked in the mirror, "I don't know who I'm looking at anymore". I do believe age comes with wisdom. So if with that, comes changes sometimes in your physical appearance then so be it.

I'm willing to accept the challenge. Because I know nothing in life remains the same. My life has been an interesting journey. It's amazing how life, can bring beauty and pain. In some seasons at the same time. think sometimes why it has to be so much pain. Why people lives are taken so easily and others exceed above and beyond all boundaries.

But God says to lean not to our own understanding. Some things will never be understood. It's all just a part of the plan. As I write this book, I can't help but to reflect on so many experiences I've shared in life. God personally has allowed me the experience to be able to shout for joy and my heart has been so broken, I felt like a knife was stabbing me inwardly. The more you walk with God, the more pain you will encounter. But the beauty is, the pain will never last forever.

CHAPTER 4

"A New Start"

After officially divorcing my husband. I eventually started a job and found me an apartment. I proceeded to move forward, and not look back to what was behind me. My ex-husband proceeded with wanting to visit our son, in hopes it seems of wanting to secretly regain our relationship. Once I told him that we were better off co-parenting, I noticed he never called or visited our son anymore.

I even remembered losing my brother during this time and asking could he watch our son. He told me he couldn't, to take our son to daycare and he wasn't able to go to funeral since he didn't put his clothes in the cleaners. I realized I had connected to an emotionless man and I needed to pursue to fully escape from him and gain my life back.

Although I could say he wasn't physically abusive he definitely was emotionally. Before divorce, we were married and it lasting a short time of nearly three years. During the time frame of our marriage, our son Journey was born. At the time this was why we were trying to make our marriage work. Obviously it still didn't work. Afterwards

I started witnessing things I couldn't understand or explain. Than during the final process of his abandonment, and leaving our child for good. I was at a loss for words. While trying to handle all that I could. It was so much physical and emotional weight, he left on me to carry and handle alone. In which included numerous psychiatrists, psychological, regular doctor appointments, activities, all while attending two colleges trying to complete my finals classes for my bachelor's degree.

I even remember his family member saying she was instructed to not watch our son from him. So I was left trying not to lose my job, with last minute daycare cancellation calls. In which she still helped watch with him when she could. I became very overwhelmed with the pressure with all I had to deal with.

As time continued, I started to notice things with our child that was becoming un-normal. Suddenly our son became unable to walk for no explainable reason. The doctor to this day still can't explain why this situation occurred. His leg had actually turned sideways and he was walking with a lymph. The condition he had come all of a sudden.

I would also receive several calls regarding his behavior at school. Due to his medical condition and these multiple daycares, claimed they couldn't handle him and asked me to pick him up. **More spiritual attacks on my child.**

Shortly after this, he had two seizures, both in the middle of the night. Once I had to rush him to the hospital. They later realized he had nerve disorders and had to undergo brain testing. His father did come around and said he would take off work to attend his procedure. However I received a text saying he knew he was a strong little boy. While under anesthesia, his father decided he wasn't going to make it.

I just remember putting the phone down in disbelief and trying to remain strong and calm for my son. After these tests his 'psychologist confirmed he had neurological nerve disorders conditions and they were genetically inherited from his father. That included extensive ADHD. His doctor advised me to enter him into a special needs school due to his erratic impulsive disruptive behavior and his mental conditions at the time. Due to his behavior, he became worse, so I became overwhelmed.

Both my parents were deceased and I didn't have anyone to immediately turn to for help. I was recently on the dean's list, but now failing my last few classes before graduation. I worked so hard for years in school, and was losing grip due to these vast distractions. All my years of hard work seem to be going down the drain.

My life was seeming to be shattered. While the last school, I placed Journey seemed to be giving up on him and saying I may need to try other options. While he was constantly being written up each day, I would receive calls from CPS, saying I wasn't administering his medicine and not even taking care of him correctly.

Anybody that really knew me, knew I followed up with all his appointments and current with all his records. He was always well dressed and taken care of. To this day I believe someone was making all these calls on me out of spite. I was constantly being harassed by this system. This has been happening since my oldest son was young and even then, they would contact me while I was planning funeral arrangements for my mother. Every finding was ruled out. This system has harassed me nearly half of my life with raising both my children.

However, this last call I received from them, after all previous cases were closed. To make matters even worse, this took my life in a sincere direction of distress, destruction and hell like I have never embarked before. It's like someone was personally using their access to this system to try to ultimately destroy me for once and for all.

After this last encounter with CPS they took my youngest while he was at school. They claimed I abandoned him, then they changed the story. I just remember everything I worked so hard for was now being taken away. I became so weak nearly lost 30 pounds in one week, due to what all was being done to me. I became isolated and felt so defeated.

It seems like my life was flashing right before my very eyes. One day I remember asking God, was I going to make it through this. I had insomnia and very stressed out. From all of my troubles, I was encountering I eventually found myself in a hospital bed from so much distress they caused me. I have a dear friend that worked for the system that suggested to me to pursue legal actions against them. Since I was denied my constitutional rights and bullied through the process.

This torment ended up being a yearly long battle that I gradually built my strength up through Christ and refused to lose. I see my children as my legacy and I refuse to give up on my boys. My mother always taught me to never give up on your kids. Near her dying day, she carried my brother his sack lunch for work with her frail ill body.

Sadly cancer had returned for the 3rd time. I am still admired how she found the strength in her body to still meet her son with his sack lunch. All while she was feeling so ill, and could hardly walk.

Again, this showed the dedication of how we love our children and willing to go to the end of the earth to support them. I am no different. No matter what others may say, I would lay my life down for my boys. In order for them to live a better life that they may fulfill their God given purpose.

I was then randomly ordered to take drug tests. When I have never done drugs in my entire life.

I can recall a doctor telling me, she couldn't believe I never turned to drugs for a release. Especially with all of life's pain I had endured. I politely told her I turned to God. They can take this earthly stuff away, but they couldn't take my faith away. In which was deeply embedded deep down into my soul. My counselor released me from ongoing counseling, but the system tried to continue repeat for no apparent reason.

This seemed personal with all they were trying to do. There wasn't any reason to extend my services, but yet they did it. While not being able to explain why. They placed my son life in possible danger. When they were called out for it, they begin to change the beat of their drum and begin to back paddle and release prior allegations.

One day I called them to follow up on some information. I immediately was forced to pull over to cry. I was wondering what was wrong with my 4-year-old son. The supervisor told me he was meaning to call me, but he didn't. Told me to calm down, and once I did, he would speak with me and hung up the phone on me. Immediately I called him back, and he shared my son was placed in a mental ward because he seemed to be "demonically possessed". I broke down crying again and felt like I couldn't breathe anymore. Knowing that my 4-year-old son was having to experience such deep horrifying experiences was beyond words could describe.

I felt like I was living in a nightmare dream and couldn't wake up. Any professional I spoke with, had never heard of someone doing a young child like this. Without a record for validating this type of response. The location they placed him, was for grownups and unimaginably horrible for a small child to be located for an entire week.

It actually negatively impacted him from being there. Shortly after, the exact same facility, was closed down and sued for mistreatment to its patients. This is location the system had placed my four year old child. I had to grasp for air, with what I was hearing and watching on the news. I later realized this system had taken all of my funding, my child was receiving from me.

They stopped the abandoning father with criminal charges against him, for having to pay child support and actually returned the money back to him. No one could explain these actions the system allowed. For some reason, they were obvious bias towards him. They did not make him follow any service plans or tests. For what true reasons was the system condoning this type of behavior.

Even through all of this pain, and wrongful treatment, I still found my way to the Potter's House Church. I couldn't wait to lift my hands and praise my God, every chance I could get. I was either going to cave in to the misery or cry out to God for help.

During this time, God allowed me to see who people really were in my life. I was able to see the real betrayers, and manipulators and naysayers. It opened up my eyes to a new dimension of my new reality. I never knew going through so much pain, I would realize such great revelation.

This is why purging was good for my spiritual, eye and soul. I thank God during this time. My uncle Joe, and his wife was there to help me. Joe is my uncle that stuck in there with me, like no one else. I will be forever grateful for the love and support he's shown. It wasn't easy to take this task on. My church also was very supportive to me during this difficult time. I will never forget the phone calls, the heartfelt prayers and support groups. I could count on for needed strength during this time in my life. Due to the grace of God, and attending numerous court sessions, and overcoming traps, plots and lies, the enemy threw at me and tried to destroy me with. God stepped right in and my son was released from this generational curse. That unfortunately his father had to grow up in and seemed to be hindered by.

God once again, worked it out for my good! Once I picked my child up, I couldn't stop hugging him. It was no concern in my mind that God delivered us from this evil. It was a test, to show how he can sustain us, even while we go through the storms of life. As long as we continue to trust and keep the faith in him, he will always make a way.

I have never seen that fail, or the righteous be forsaken. I now enjoy sharing my story, in hopes it will inspire and encourage others that are going through their storms. God can bring you out! I know I've been through the fire, for more than just myself. I went through the flames to tell you, God was with me the entire time. He never left my side.

I made it out! Guess what, you are next! I can relate when people are constantly watching you. They quick to persecute, condemn and disown and talk about you. Don't worry about it! God will change and fix that too!

I am a living witness and a walking testimony that persevere for God, opens up closed doors. God continually told me, fight like a good solider. Then after you've suffered a while, I will renew you. You can still walk out of the ashes with victory! You can come out of the fire that was meant to destroy you! Last but not least, again my purpose for sharing my story, is to hopefully help someone overcome similar tragedies and challenges they are trying to defeat alone. To please know, you can't fight this battle alone. You need God help to survive it! It can consist of spiritually, mentally, financially, emotionally or physically. However it may be.

I have endured and survived it only by the grace and mercy of God being in my life. My life has been through so many twists and turns. I don't have enough emotions to express them all. Even as things around me are constantly shifting. I can honestly attest that God is the only, that remains consistently the same through it all! He has been my constant life jacket during all personal turbulence and life troubles.

CHAPTER 5

Finding Myself

Going through these emotions it caused me to sometimes feel like I couldn't win from losing. So I was stuck in the crossroads. It can come a time you can become so broken and misunderstood you enter into a deep soul search. It made me begin to question the reasons of why. My emotions were on a roller coaster with trying to make sense of everything and balance everything out.

It seems as if everything was attacking me at once. I know if I didn't fill my spiritual being up, I would begin to be consumed and darkness was steadily trying to take me over and out. Out of 43 years I have never experienced the types of attacks, I was experiencing. It seems everything was coming at me like a whirlwind tornado and looking to destroy and cut up anything that was left breathing. Especially since I had literally lost everything. Including my home, car, savings and any valuable assets that were remaining.

I heard the devil constantly telling me to give up. To complete the mission by taking myself out of my own misery.

Every time I took two steps forward, he made sure I was knocked down five steps backwards. He used his entire arsenal to try and sabotage my life meaning. But God! I couldn't help but to constantly ask myself, why I am being fought like this on this level. I had to think back and remember from my past. Higher levels new devils.

Normally if he is fighting me like this, it has to be for some kind of strong reason. He is not fighting me this hard, like this for absolutely nothing. This is what made me roll up my sleeve, and get back in the ring with my red covered in the blood boxing gloves. To start strategizing my swing for one good final punch, to knock him out like never before!

I must admit, its hard thinking about clarity and grasping a greater understanding, when you are going through great attacks. You normally have only the strength to go through it sometimes that is even a test. No less than trying to fully understand the fight you are in. But if you are wise you will. For example, it's like fighting and swinging with your eyes closed. Sometimes you need to know which way you are swinging, so you can make sure your aims are knocking out deep rooted targets that are trying to defeat you. It does come a time, when you just have to look the enemy in the face, and say no devil, you're not having this this! I don't care if it's your promise, child, marriage, vision, home, business, etc.

If he is trying to take you as down as far as possible. Hoping you are so low; you won't have the strength to keep going. But that's when you have to cling on for dear life, and access that second wind of air and rise for the occasion of victory. Like your life depends on it. However, if you think about it, it literally does.

The promises of God is yes and amen!

Right when the enemy think he is about to take you out for the kill, rise up like Gillian army and show that snake what you are really made of. It will leave him confused and totally mistaken. Thinking you will just lie down and not fight for yourself and what God promised you can have.

You haven't survived all that you have for nothing. The devil is a liar! You didn't overcome hell and high water to sank and not survive. He has underestimated you for the last time, and now it's time to show what you are really made of! While you are walking through your seasons, God will be with you, to bring you out as pure gold. Just watch and see, it's totally different when you see it with your own eyes.

The wonderful manifestation he is entering you into for his glory. You will know it when it arrives! I've never seen the righteous forsaken, neither asking for begging bread. Therefore, keep going and pressing towards the mark. It's closer than you think.

You may endure great pain and even agony at times. But really, the joy of the Lord is your true strength and your refuge in time of trouble. So believe in that and hold that near your heart during these trying times. The word says, God is close to the brokenhearted. So he really is right there with you. Don't underestimate the wonders of his power.

The blood has the ability to carry you like nothing else. I have tried it and know; this is why I wanted to share my story with you and tell you what I know actually works. Continue on with your armor of God, and keep fighting on this traitorous battlefield. Because with God on your side, you will win!!!

I would also notice with my personal experiences, it seems when life seems more trying and things appear to be getting worse. That's when out of nowhere a special text or call may suddenly appear. When I want to drop my head and say Lord pass this cup. Suddenly by an unexpected surprise. I had to lift it up my head, to answer a new update.

I am proud to say, that that phone call or text that happened to arrive. Brought a sudden relief and or smile on my face. It took me away from the heaviness or burdens I was dealing with. This is why I strongly believe, God will not allow you to handle more than you can bare.

He knows the perfect timing when to intervene and make a way. It seems, God was teaching me how to anchor the winds of the storm with some turbulence, but sunshine still appears throughout the sky. It actually allowed me to value balance while dealing with adversity.

While dealing with life anything can possibly happen. Just continue to keep your hand in God hand. He can lead and guide you through it all every step of the way. As the many times my grandmother will tell me, she never seen that fail. Meaning the power of God, and all his great works and wonders. Some of my toughest battles included some of my greatest victories. Rather it was regarding my personal life encounters or career opportunities. God stepped in and turned it around in my favor. Once again, the righteous will not be forsaken. I want you to repeat these words, and get it down heavily in your spirit.

All things are indeed possible with Christ Jesus on your side. The ride may seem bumpy at times, but if you just allow yourself to get snug and hold on. The ride will become smooth sailing. It will begin to flow as living water. You shall see the salvation of the Lord dearly over your life. Sometimes I had to grit my teeth. But watch God use that same grit for greatness. I'm happy for you!

You can't fight this good fight of life alone. I needed to step back and God to help me. At times it requires help from others. It's nothing wrong with realizing you can't handle everything alone. In which I use to always try to do.

Its funny how as life progresses, and time continues to move, it changes the definition of what you thought and even expected for your life. We all are in this journey together trying to meet and fulfill our God given purpose in life. We all have so many gifts and talents to step into. Sometimes it takes others sharing their personal experiences, to help enlighten us on what we need to be doing.

Even if it only just helps us to avoid certain mistakes, while pressing towards a better place in life. Knowledge is power. It can help in so many ways. It's sad to me; people rather keep life changing information to themselves.

Rather than helping to improve the lives of others. I see that as selfish and insecure. Many can be threatened or intimidated, by how God can raise you to your next level. Therefore, they rather not help you with anything. Hoping you won't figure things out since they want help you. It's disturbing when you have to witness this personally.

It's enough greatness for everyone to win. This is why I love God. No one can curse what he has blessed. Vice versa. No one can bless what he has cursed. He says he is closer to you than a brother.

He is more with you, than the world is against you. So, with this being said. Just keep going! You are not alone. It is people cheering for you! Like myself, hoping and believing that God will get the sincere victory out of your life!

It's not about us; it's about passing the torch and helping others. We are all just passing through the forever changing shifting world. Why not help the next person out. Especially if you know and have experienced what they may be going through. This just seems to be the right thing to do towards others. God can bless you for having a humble compassionate heart for others.

If you think about it, that's exactly what he has done for us. Life would not be the same without his presence. It seems many people forget how he loved us, and waited on us, to get to where we are today. We didn't get here on our own. It took the realization of knowing how great God is and all the many things he did for us.

Many arrived due to the testimony of others. Sharing the goodness of how God intervened in their lives. Or some may had a personal encounter of tragedy. However and whatever brought you to the cross, I'm glad you made it!

This world is not an easy place to live in. But with God on your side, the navigation device that he equips us with, keeps us and protect us like nothing else in this world. This is why I am so thankful. It's hard to imagine how I made it before connecting and living with God in my life.

There are certain times and things in your life, you can't help but to say, it's no way I could have gotten through that season of my life, without the mighty hand of God! It was definitely a fainting and collapsing moment where the Holy Spirit intervened. This is why I praise God and continuously give God the glory!

The more you endure the trials and struggles of life, the easier your praise will become. Since you know without a shadow of doubt, he was the only one that brought you over and out.
Ok, it's ok to shout right here with your victory dance. Glory hallelujah!

Needless to say, life is about cycles. Since it's important for me to try to live my best life possible. I try not to repeat mistakes or repeat bad cycles from my past. I know this is significant so the devil can't win. If the devil can keep you stuck and repeating the same vicious cycle that keeps you from elevating to your promise than he will.

This is why it is important to learn from your mistakes and move on. I know this can be easier said than done. Normally the reasons why people get caught up in this vicious cycle, is it's convenient and comfortable. You don't have to step into the unknown not knowing what to expect. We all have been there at times.

But it's our faith in God that helps to launch us into our next dimension in life. This is where our trust function kicks in with our navigational tool. We have to keep pressing higher to the mark.

It does takes great discipline and focused determination. Endurance and dedication to God smells like rain. This is why we must maintain and keep the faith. Put your worship hands up. It's time to praise God in spirit and in truth!

CHAPTER 6

The Loan

I use to wonder was it a limit to our faith. Especially since some people appear to be dreamers, where others seem to be limited with their thinking. Again, God will never mislead us or forsake us. He says, have faith of a mustard seed. If you have never seen a mustard seed, you might want to go look at one. You will see they are not that large.

So in other words, it doesn't take a huge amount of faith to believe. It's very similar to the practice of mind over matter. Being able to keep your mind on Jesus, in spite of the circumstances you are going through is the key.

Once your trust is established in him, this can open the door to freedom and liberty that you need in your life. It will begin to provide a peace that passes all understanding. For example, I find myself amazed how certain things I go through don't make me want to become unraveled. I can easily recall once when it did. I knew it had to be the peace of God to allow me to continue to stand and go through certain things at times even with a smile.

I even had to take a second look at myself and be like "ok God". I must be operating through your strength. I knew if I had to depend on mine, I would have collapsed with all the pressure. Who wouldn't serve a God like this? His protection and love for us is endless. This is why I am not ashamed to confess his goodness and hopefully inspire, whomever I can to seek and follow him.

Your life will change for the better because of it. It will never be the same, since connecting to God's unlimited greatness. I have seen times where I have gone and applied for things. That could consist of accounts to cars. Stay with me now!

I knew my credit and resources may not have been the best, to apply for these things at the time. However, it was specific needs that I had. But once I received in my spirit, to go forth and apply, my knees may have shook some. I begin to ask God, was I hearing him correctly.

Even after I just talked to him about it. It's amazing how our minds can play tricks on us if we let it! I begin to immediately just think back to God did hear me. The only thing I could do is step out on faith. So, I proceeded with the applications. Obviously knowing not what to expect. Including knowing I might not match the criteria of what the requirements asked for. This made me more nervous!

But totally just surrendering and trusting God, that in some kind of way something good will happen. Keep in mind, after applying and these organizations looking at my information, I didn't meet their criteria. The faith in me still stood. Believing in what God told me, I continued to wait around to see what would happen.

I am still surprised and taken back by how miraculous things shifted for me. These examples are best with different illustrations. One that included a vehicle and the other starting my own ministry with funding resources. That I both needed at the time, in order to help me with the everyday functions of my life.

The power of the Lord, is all that I can say! I am so pleased, that I met God criteria! He brought me through once again. I can remember that day, the dealership phone line continued to remain busy. It seems like no matter when I called that day, I received a busy signal. Even the lady that worked there couldn't believe how their phone system was acting up. Not only where they not able to receive calls, but they were not able to call out themselves.

Now I had to say to myself, normally when weird or strange activity is happening. The breakthrough must be on the other side. My spiritual side knows that something is trying to happen to block me. This is my confirmation that something else good can arise. I know many people can attest to what I'm speaking about. It's normally just nothing more than a sure sign that your blessing is on its way! So, get ready! When the devil is mad like that, he is trying to interfere and block whatever it is you have going on.

So finally, when the phones proceeded to work, I did receive a call from higher management in the company. Listen! That not only was my loan fully approved with no money down. I had a choice to the one I wanted. I think I could have cried and laughed at the same time. Let's just say the options were higher than what I asked for or could imagine. So, it's no way, you can't tell me God isn't watching over his children! When you trust in God, and step out on faith, God will simply blow your mind! Sometimes he will test us, to see that we really do believe. Along with my new ministry, God revealed strategies to me I couldn't even comprehend that was even possible. I just activated my faith. I set up meetings with management as advised to do, along with following the instructions given me.

From this point on, I begin to receive funding for assistance to help me with growing my business and writing my first book. That I am totally blessed to do and what you are reading right now. I simply just kept the faith, no matter what I was experiencing.

Listened and followed God's divine strategy and guess what the rest is history! This is why I can't stop saying, who wouldn't serve a God like this! My life has never been the same since I entered into his goodness. It is the best decision I have ever made in my entire life!!!

CHAPTER 7

The Knockout

Today I have been thinking about all I have had to overcome in life. I sometimes want to feel happy and sometimes even sad. Feeling overjoyed with what I'm seeing God do. Sometimes feeling sad, about the people that were dear to my heart, I lost along the way. Who wasn't able to share the victories with me here on earth.

For example, like my mother. But I know she is still watching me. I know it would make her proud to know, that I kept my faith in God. I didn't get lost in remain stuck in the distractions and schemes, the devil tried to use to hinder me. Even with worldly systems and trying to mess with my children. I followed her path, with not giving up on my kids. I overcame the pain that tried to shatter my love for living for Christ. I would do it again if I had to.

Her strength was carried over and deposited into me. It's one of the best deposits I have ever received.

Only by God's saving grace and mercy, that continued to give me the divine strength to maintain. Especially when my flesh was torn and tired. This is where true hope comes from. This is that turning in your soul when you know, that better days have to come. Even when you don't see them. It's that beat in your heart and balling up your fist. Only displaying your undying strength for true happiness.

On my darkest, loneliest day, I can find that hope in Him. In your darkest loneliest days, you have to have some kind of reason of hope for yourself. Without that hope you can easily become unraveled and feel defeated. When you feel that you are becoming unraveled or starting to feel defeated, always know it must be something good that is trying to happen.

Think back and try to find and hold on to a memory that brings a smile to your face. It can be as simple as when someone acted friendly towards you on your drive home, paid a small bill for you, or when something positive distracted you from your pain.

Has there ever been a time when you were so worried about how things would work out, but in the end, you didn't have to because somehow it worked out where you didn't have to. Have you ever witnessed something like this happening?

In times of pain, remembering these moments can sustain you. It's so many things that can cause you to feel discouraged. Hold on to the positive energy instead envision something you want to do and what steps needed, to put a plan into action.

This can jumpstart your vision and help make your dream a reality. God can prosper your vision and leave you speechless. It can be an easy task starting out. So start off with a simple step; just write it down on paper. Start visualizing what you want to happen.

Try using tools and research on what you need to start doing, to help bring your dream to a reality. You may be the only one that knows the depth of your dream and understand why it means so much to you. However doing some research can let you know that you are not alone, and that others have taken steps that can help you move forward.

These small steps can help you stay in an engaging mind frame to move toward your vision. Its people waiting and needing you to complete the mark. You vision can be someone next answered prayer.

It's never too late to dream, God works in mysterious ways. He has performed miracles and will continue to "If he can pregnant Abraham and Sarah in their golden years with a child". Then surely, he is the same God that can still perform miracles in our lives. Just don't give up. My grandmother has always said, where there is a will, there is definitely a way."

Even now as I am, I'm encouraging you, I am also doing the same for myself. I encourage you to think about how you can lift yourself by lifting others. One simple word from you, can help transition someone else's move into a new direction that they couldn't see or imagine for themselves.

The scripture that says, life and death is in the power of the tongue. We choose how to use the power by choosing what we speak, since they are powerful enough to help change our destiny of life. This is why I choose to try to stay positive, rather than speak negativity to possibly stagnate my blessings.

It's not that you don't have anything to say. We all know life isn't always easy. It's not that things don't go wrong, and you can't say something regarding it. It's just that how we speak, can change the atmosphere of what can happen. So choosing to see the positive and speak energy into that positivity can lead you to taking a higher approach, in how you are able to choose to handle certain things.

It takes discipline and maturity to help tame your emotions and your words. However, with God, timing, and self-discipline, anything can be possible to those who truly believe. Put one foot in front of the other. Expect good things will happen. God will give you everything you need to see you through.

Don't worry, everything you are going through is simply just a part of the process. I'm sure you may have heard this before. It is true, it will make you better and help others out because of it. You are needed and was made for such a times as this! The tests are to only prepare your strength for all the many meaningful wonderful plans Jesus has for your life.

Final Words

I want to close this memoir, by giving my final words of encouragement to those who has a story similar or even totally different from mine. It's not that things don't go wrong and you can't do something regarding it. It's just how we process and speak, can change the atmosphere of what can possibly happen.

So choosing to see the higher road, that positivity can lead you to taking a higher approach, in how you are able to handle certain situations. Just don't never give up and hold on to Gods unchanging words for dear life! He will give you the grace and mercy to endure, the strength to survive, and the hope for a better future.

Your faith is essential for this journey. Guard your mind and soul at all cost, when the enemy comes in like a flood, and try to tear you down don't stop from receiving what god has for you. Listen! He faithfully and consistently takes very good care of all his people. So I've included some scriptures that hopefully will be helpful to you. These scriptures helped me to get through some of my toughest seasons throughout my life. In my southern voice, it's the grease for those squeaky wheels, that's sometimes needed to help weather the storm.

My southern 101 year old grandmother would tell me, you might give out, but never give up! So even at times where I thought I was fainting in midair, God came and caught me! God never changes. Now we may change at some point. That's sometimes inevitable with life.

But I am more than thankful that he remains consistent at all times. He is indeed a solid rock that we can stand on at all times. If we simply just trust in him and believe no matter what we are going through. Keep a little piece of faith in your heart and watch and see God move on your behalf.

I am a living witness to what I am saying. The righteous will rise above. I'm so glad we can hold God to his word, and talk to him about it and he will honor it, and make good of it some kind of way.

He may not come when you want him, but he is still always right on time! I have a smirk on my face, while finishing up my story. It's nearly eleven o'clock at night. I've been writing literally all day long. Just thinking about the outpouring over God's goodness. That's why I can't stop writing.

I was convicted to finish my story for you. I was lead and felt the Holy Spirit tugging on me, telling me you have a story to share daughter. That is actually a little overdue. So when the father speaks, I'm honored to listen. Since he is such a good father and knows what we need.

This is what inspired me to open up my personal life book and pour out from it. I want you to learn from my mistakes. Don't be deceived by traps set up to hinder and destroy you from fulfilling your destiny and dreams in life. The devil will use whatever he can to try to keep you from discovering, your milk and honey in the land.

I believe the more equipped you are with recognizing his arsenal, you will be better prepared with knowing how to defeat it. It will give you a better knowledge in knowing what to look for in people and situations. Awareness is key to developing your understanding for what is needed to be known.

This is why the blood of Jesus is needed to cover all areas of life.

Continue to press and pursue the Holy Spirit to enter in and intervene on your behalf. Allow it to proceed and go before you and willingly follow its lead.

I gladly live by this scripture, when my daddy whispers to me to go forth, I proceed with this needed scripture in mind. Isaiah 54:17 King James Version (KJV) "No weapon that is formed against thee shall prosper; and every tongue that shall rise against thee in judgment thou shalt condemn. This is the heritage of the servants of the Lord, and their righteousness is of me, saithe the Lord."

I noticed in the bible how Joseph was mishandled and disowned by his very own siblings. I can't but help to feel the same way when I think about the betrayal I felt. As mentioned, I do strongly believe if God didn't fully give or ordained you to someone or something, you are operating out of place.

That can negatively affect what you put your hands to and can create unfortunate consequences you possibly have to live out.

Throughout my life, I have learned to obey God and yes, it has been through a series of trials and error. Sometimes life will teach you lessons that sometimes we as humans are unwilling to adhere to. I've learned to bow down to his will, since it has proven to be the ultimate best way for my life. My love for Jesus makes me want to do better.

Since after all, love does conquer all. So with all the life changing advice revealed to me, it all begins to make sense now. These are the times when we need to encourage each other, while shining our lights for Jesus!

About Author

Follow Me

Instagram: jonestreka

Email: beautifullybruisedlj@gmail.com

Please visit my website at
amazon.com/author/latrekajones

Booking Speaking Engagements Contact Info

La Treka Jones,
Daddy Lights Ministry, Po Box 24424, Fort Worth, Texas 76124
daddylights.ministry@yahoo.com

More about the Author

La Treka Jones is a single mother who has been able to overcome many adversaries to become the light force she is today. After years of dealing with abuse, rejection and abandonment of her and her special needs child, La Treka has been able to use her experience as a platform to motivate and inspire.

La Treka has been able to overcome homelessness, financial hardship, and mental anguish all while putting in the work. La Treka's saving grace was the ability to not ask "Why me, Lord?" but to say "Use me, Lord". She knows whole heartily that her faith and steadfastness is what was able to bring her to where she is now. She knows it was God's grace and mercy that brought her through life's constant opposition.

The Motivational Coach

La Treka's goal is to motivate all people, from all walks of life. Including children with special needs, and to be a resource to parents and caregivers, for these gifted individuals. She has normally used her life as an open platform to help motivate and challenge others to reach their full potential. Her strengths and passion go hand and hand with her dedication to provide needed solutions. La Treka is primary known for her creative ways in connecting with people. She is great with reaching the unreachable and making them feel worthy of their God given gifts. La Treka is a frequent speaker and loves inspiring others with her heartfelt delivery and compassionate interactions.

Appearances

La Treka Jones has appeared on numerous television shows and productions. Including but not limited to being featured on the Book of John Gray Show, (Oprah Winfrey Network) Steve Harvey Talk show, The View Talk show, Queen Latifah Show and featured on The Potter's House Church "Bishop TD Jakes" Best Buddies Special Interview.

Special Moments in my life

My grandmother and mother

My sons Courtlend and Journey

I was a guest on the Steve Harvey Show.

Pastor John and his wife Aventer Gray

Divine Strategies from God

I started my own organization with faith and not giving up on my vision. I didn't have any clue how it would happen. But I knew some kind of way it could. I was a single mother that believed in more than my current situation. I didn't have the money or the resources to start a business. But I refused to allow that to stop me from trying. I remembered one day, hearing a small inner voice telling me to step out on faith. I begin to realize I would never know my destiny, by remaining where I was. Shortly afterwards, I scheduled my first meeting with a Walmart manager. I was extremely nervous while waiting to meet the store manager that day.

The meeting that extended over to the rest of my life. That included an offer to help me launch my new ministry. It's amazing how only one moment can literally define the hands of time. God thank you, for providing the strategy and trusting me to see it through. That small clear voice is absolutely stunning. I am a living witness that faith and action can spring forth opportunities you could have never imagined.

Special Recognition to Parents & Caregivers with Special Needs Children

My heart salutes your superior dedication and care for your loved ones. I have a special place in my heart for you all! My youngest son is considered a special needs child and requires consistent care. I've noticed these children are so gifted and talented in so many different ways.

For example, my son deals with triggers that affects his sensory, but he is excellent at drawing and great at retaining information. Keep in mind they are truly scholars like no one else. His love for others is endless. He loves giving hugs and trying to make others feel special.

One day while picking him up while sitting in the crib he couldn't stand on his legs. I kept wondering how he can go to bed walking and wake up unable to do so. I refused to accept whatever games or plots the enemy was trying to play. I knew something was very strange with what I was witnessing. It seems like he started trying to walk but it was with a limp. I immediately contacted his primary doctor and made him an appointment to be seen.

I proceeded to take him to the nursery then I proceeded with my work activities. Shortly later that day, I received a call that my youngest seem to be losing his balance. He started to cry since his legs wasn't moving correctly. I remember thanking her for calling me and I went to go pick him up.

I proceeded to take him to the doctor early and the physician met with him. She was also at a loss for words and didn't understand how and why his leg seemed to be turned outwards. He was not able to gain his balance.

She begins to order some tests and asked me to follow up with a specialist to help detect the problem. After running several tests, the doctors asked had anything of this sort ever occurred in our family before and I explained that it had not. The doctor proceeded to tell me to continue to watch Journey with his leg and record his movements.

Therefore, we proceeded on with our day, while I was watching him move around the house. I didn't understand how can a child almost three years old have no experience of any fall or hurt, but suddenly have a leg that is turned in a totally different direction that causes him not to walk. When I tell you, the spiritual warfare is real! We must continue to keep the faith and don't accept anything that doesn't agree with your spirit.

Continuing to observe my child and pray, the following morning we went to church. My oldest son went with us and while leaving out of service, he said mama his leg seems to be an abnormal size than before. I continued to pray and watch Journey, eventually his leg repositioned itself. It returned back in its rightful position.

This was confirmed when afterwards he started running and playing outside. This immediately gained my attention; I couldn't do nothing but be grateful about his progress I witnessed in front of my very eyes. To God be the glory! While watching his facial expression he couldn't understand what was happening with everything.

But God once again worked it out for our good. I must admit it seemed like my child was under some sort of spiritual warfare attack. Even since he was first born. This again, is why I admire all who knows what it's like to care for those in special need. The responsibilities are not easy but obtainable.

The work at times can seem tiresome and even overwhelming. But the beauty is, God will never put more on you than you can handle. Even when it seems like the devil is trying to come in like a flood. You have to remain calm and positive and realize you are not alone in this battle. God loves you and knows exactly what to do in his perfect timing to turn your situation around.

You have been given great strength and compassion to help care for those in need. Who are living with challenges that most couldn't relate to! I applaud you for being you. You need to be celebrated and know how much we care about you. Your assistance will not be unrecognized and you are not alone.

Having a child with special needs require time and attention around the clock. Due to all the time and effort it takes to help raise these children, I know personally it takes a special type of person to handle the many multi-tasks.

 Congratulations! God trusted you to be capable to fulfill the position. Anyone couldn't handle what you do. I find it amazing to connect and talk to the people that can. You are so extraordinary and don't never forget it. Thank you again, for all that you effortless continue to do.

I know every day is not always the same raising special gifted children. Some days can go as expected; however, some days can be considered difficult. I know with my son with his nerve disorder, it can cause him to become easily disgruntled and defiant with his behavior. He does not like change and thrives best in a structured environment. He constantly is running and moving around. His doctor years ago says he is considered ADHD. So that's why I try to constantly keep him busy and involved in some type of sports and activities. This has really been beneficial for me. Since he does have extreme energy and hardly ever slows down.

Later on, after receiving the diagnosis, one night I woke up in the middle night to check on my youngest. I found him crying in the bed and begin to pick him up and realized his eyes, were rolling back and his arm was severely shaking. I immediately thought my son was having a seizure. I just remember holding him and trying to calm him down.

While I called the emergency number, I noticed he begin to stop shaking and his eyes appeared normal again. My youngest started to stop crying, even though I felt I wanted to start. I was so nervous from what I was experiencing. I followed up with the doctor regarding what happened, and he confirmed a seizure had occurred. So, this was another medical condition I had to be aware of moving forward. God has been my solid strength throughout everything. He definitely is my strong tower throughout my days of uncertainty.

Believe it or not the scare did not end here. I was out of town visiting my oldest son in college. While preparing for the end of a busy day, my family and I went to sleep. However, in the middle of the night, Journey started screaming. I immediately turned on the lights and picked him up and realized that he was unable to open his eyes. It seems as if his eyes were closed shut. His body appeared frail and red. It seems like every time this happens it always occurs in the middle of the night.

I grabbed my purse and headed to the nearest hospital to try to seek help. The doctor once again ran some tests and confirmed another sign of a seizure. He provided some instructions to follow up with his primary doctor and recommended some more extensive tests.

His neurologist scheduled some brain tests and scans. After waiting a few hours for Journey to come from under anesthesia. The doctor met with me with the results. He shared he didn't see any abnormal problems. By the grace of God, I rejoiced in receiving the good news. I know the results could have totally been different. My youngest has not witnessed any more seizures. It's been years since we had any kind of these encounters. I still have a very tender heart for those that do. Seizures can appear at any given time, and it is different types. You have to be ready when they appear. God knows what we go through with our children.

My youngest has really experienced some medical scares since birth. He stopped growing during birth, and suffered severe colic afterwards. He then had some physical and mental attacks. I have done nothing, but rolled up my sleeves and prepared my heart and mind for the fight. I never gave up, no matter how difficult the challenges are.

Moms, fathers, caregivers be encouraged.
Keep going! You are on a journey that is challenging but worth the sacrifice. You are making an impact in so many special hearts. I pray God continue to keep you with his joy and his strength. Let us remain determined to complete the mission that God has trusted us to do.

Thank you...

Inspiring Scriptures While Fighting Spiritual Warfare

For the word of God is living and powerful, and sharper than any two-edged sword, piercing even to the division of soul and spirit, and of joints and marrow, and is a discerner of the thoughts and intents of the heart. And there is no creature hidden from His sight, but all things are naked and open to the eyes of Him to whom we must give account. (Hebrews 4:12-13 NKJV)

But you have carefully followed my doctrine, manner of life, purpose, faith, longsuffering, love, perseverance, persecutions, and afflictions... what persecutions I endured. And out of them all the Lord delivered me.

Yes, and all who desire to live godly in Christ Jesus will suffer persecution. But evil men and impostors will grow worse and worse, deceiving and being deceived. But you must continue in the things which you have learned and been assured of, knowing from whom you have learned them, and that from childhood you have known the Holy Scriptures, which are able to make you wise for salvation through faith which is in Christ Jesus.

All Scripture is given by inspiration of God, and is profitable for doctrine, for reproof, for correction, for instruction in righteousness, that the man of God may be complete, thoroughly equipped for every good work. (2 Timothy 3:10-17 NKJV)

Don't Quit

When things go wrong, as they sometimes will,
When the road you're trudging seems all uphill,
When the funds are low and the debts are high,
And you want to smile, but you have to sigh,
When care is pressing you down a bit,
Rest, if you must, but don't you quit.

Life is queer with its twists and turns,
As every one of us sometimes learns,
And many a failure turns about,
When he might have won had he stuck it out;
Don't give up though the pace seems slow--
You may succeed with another blow.

Often the goal is nearer than,
It seems to a faint and faltering man,
Often the struggler has given up,
When he might have captured the victor's cup,
And he learned too late when the night slipped down,
How close he was to the golden crown.

Success is failure turned inside out--
The silver tint of the clouds of doubt,
And you never can tell how close you are,
It may be near when it seems so far,
So stick to the fight when you're hardest hit--
It's when things seem worst that you must not quit.

- Author unknown

References

Hebrews 4:12-1

http://www.battlefocused.org/copyright.php#NKJV

2 Timothy 3:10-17 Open in Logos Bible Software (if available) NKJV)

Do not be overcome by evil, but overcome evil with good. (Romans 12:21 NKJV)

...the battle is the LORD's... (1 Samuel 17:47 KJV)

"...the enemy... is the devil..." (Matthew 13:37-39 KJV)

"The thief does not come except to steal, and to kill, and to destroy. I have come that they may have life, and that they may have it more abundantly." (John 10:10 NKJV)

"He who is not with Me is against Me, and he who does not gather with Me scatters abroad." (Matthew 12:30 NKJV)

"...what king, going to make war against another king, does not sit down first and consider whether he is able with ten thousand to meet him who comes against him with twenty thousand? Or else, while the other is still a great way off, he sends a delegation and asks conditions of peace. So likewise, whoever of you does not forsake all that he has cannot be My disciple." (Luke 14:31-33 NKJV)

Acknowledgments

I would like to acknowledge my one hundred- and one-year old grandmother for helping to raise me. Her name is Rosie Lee Jones. She is the solid rock in our family that brings everyone together. She has strength that is simply immeasurable. She taught me how to be a lady and to never allow anything to bother me and come between my dreams. I have always admired how she wouldn't allow negativity to distract her from enjoying her life.

Her sense of humor is priceless. Her love for people is contagions and I believe this is why she is loved by so many. She has always had a heart to help people. I've never seen her turn anyone away. She has always provided divine wisdom and a smile to whoever was in need. At times, included some hot meal and financial assistance.

Last but not least I would also like to acknowledge my loving deceased mother Sylvia Lee Jones. She has always supported my dreams even when others didn't. She was my personal cheerleader at auditions and in life in general. Words cannot possibly describe how I miss her dearly! She inspired me to keep going in life and to never give up on my dreams. She would also tell me; God is an instant God! I have witnessed personally that this statement is definitely true! She would also provide me direct insight about life and some things, I'm just now able to see it come to full intuition. I am truly grateful for the time me and my mother shared, and I will never forget it! Until we meet again, I promise everything God allows me to do, I will do it for the both of us! Love you forever!

Your daughter,

LaTreka Jones

Notes Page

Notes Page

<u>Notes Page</u>

<u>Notes Page</u>

Made in the USA
Middletown, DE
04 January 2026